Things that looks like art

A short guide to a more playful and intuitive approach towards Art.

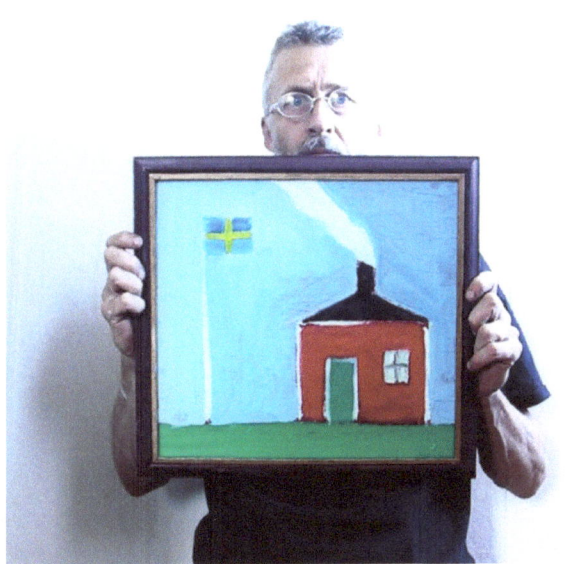

In Sweden, being of my age, you had to do a school-maturity test before entering school. One task was to draw smoke and a flag on a preprinted picture of a house with a chimney and a flagpole.
The idea was to get both the smoke and the flag pointing in the same direction.
Doing so you were considered mature enough.

Later in life I made this picture. It was when I had decided to do things that looks like Art.

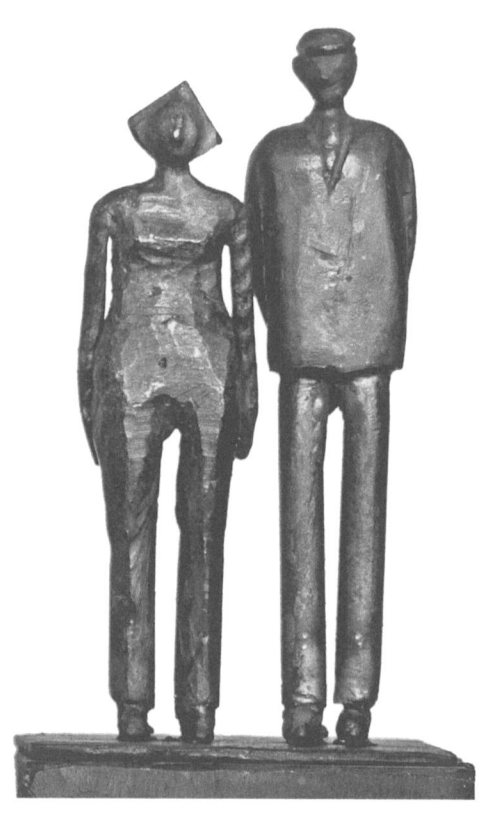

Things that looks like Art are made for a higher purpose.
Has pretensions.

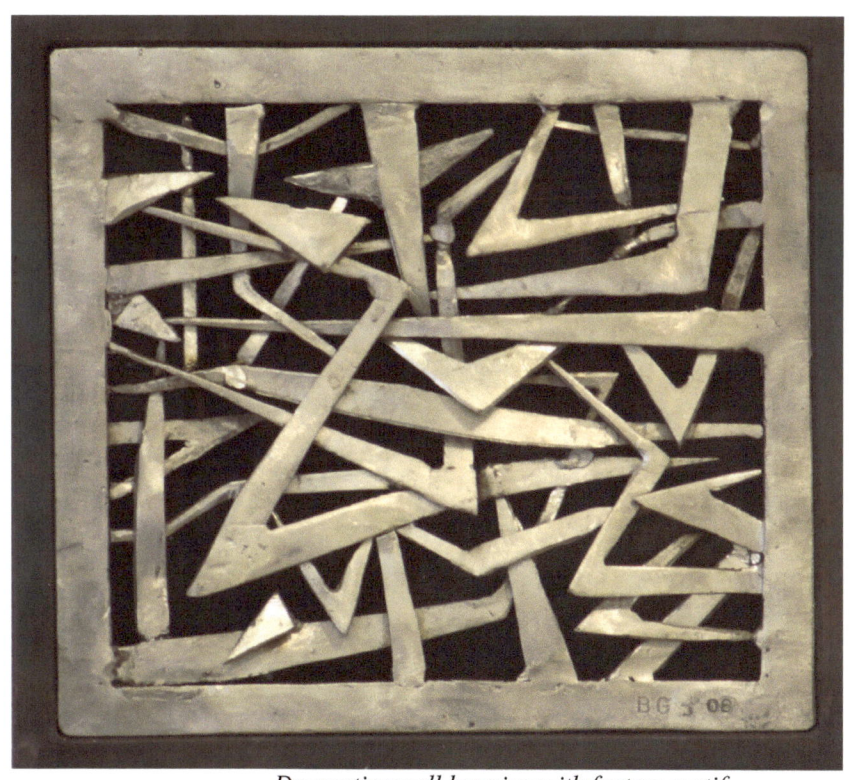

Decorative wall hanging with fantasy motif

It´s more than simple adornment.
It´s the subjective meeting with the
impressions of another human being.

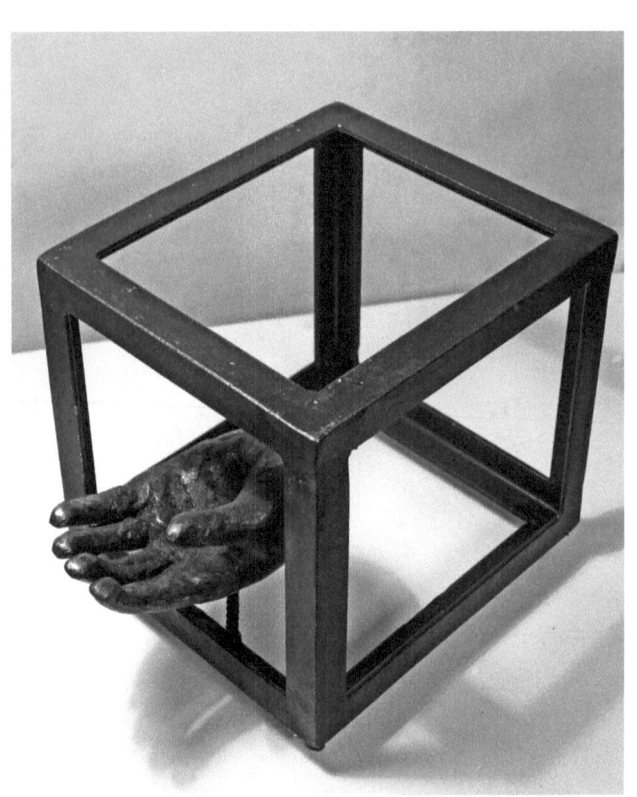

Sometimes it´s so subtle even I find it hard to follow.

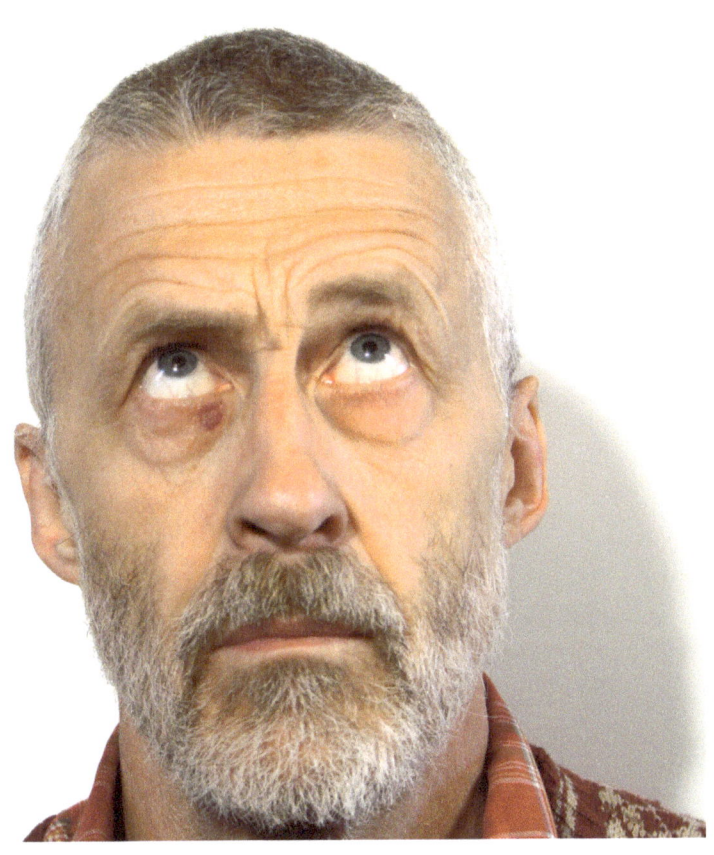

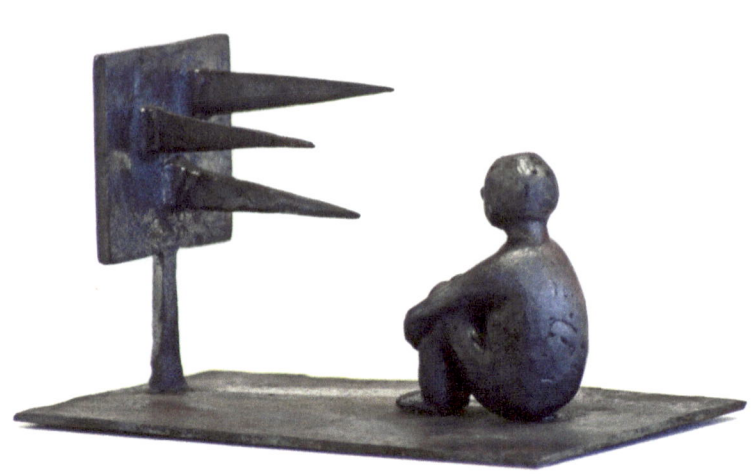

Things that looks like Art
should be felt instead
of being understood.

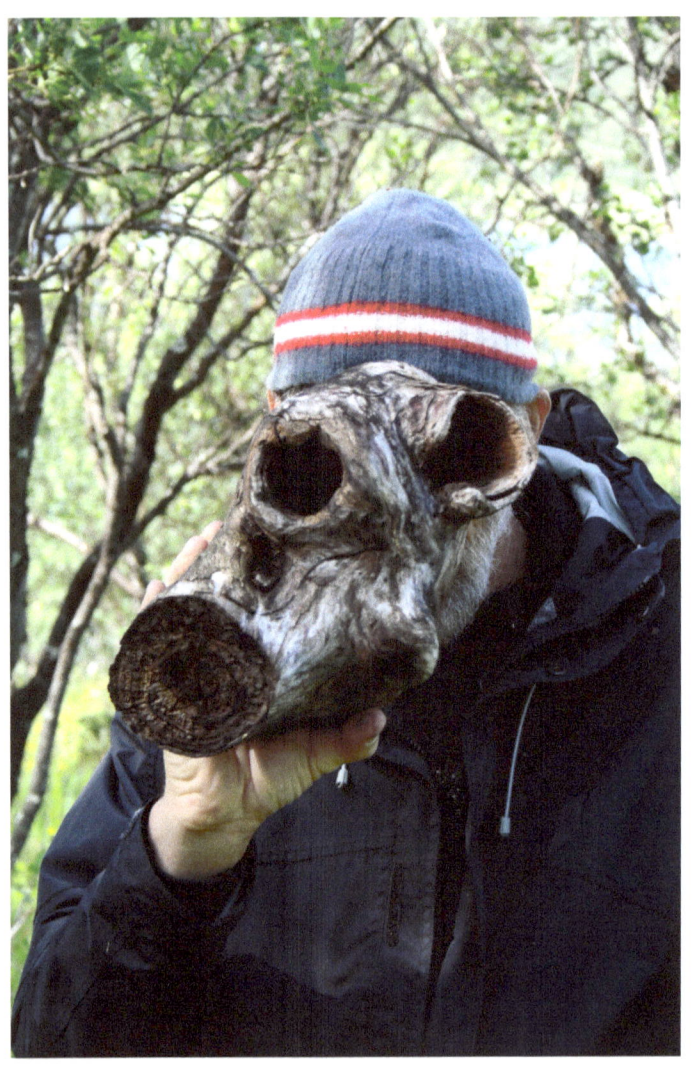

It´s a question of attitude. You have
to practice your associative ability.

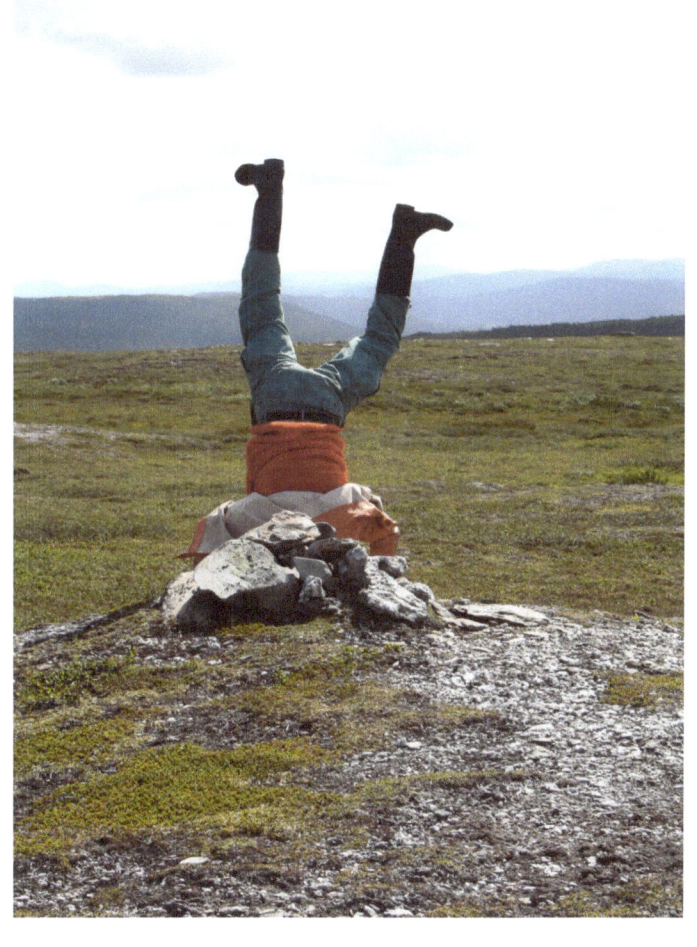

This is a way of doing it.
But it´s not right.

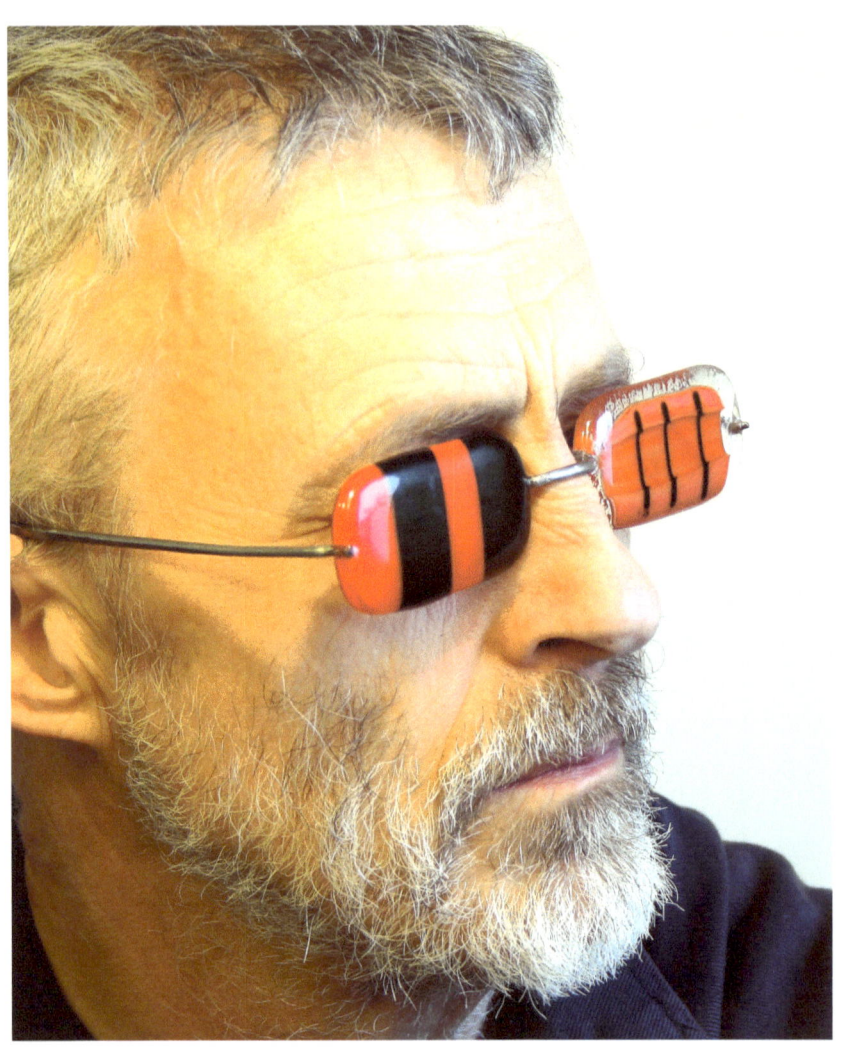

It´s better to use
Art-goggles.

With Art-goggles you see the Art in life.
Queer-glasses makes the sexual dimensions
super ordinate and with Economy-glasses
everything seem to be for sale.

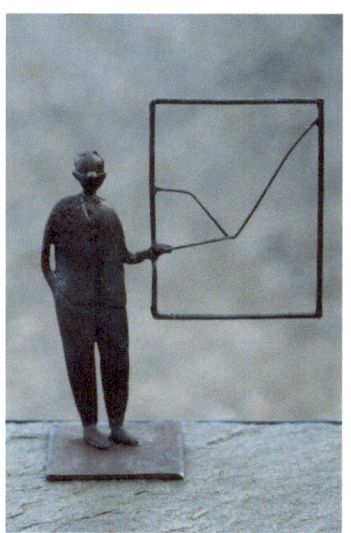

Most people wants a
manual. Something
to hold on to even if
it´s just a price list.

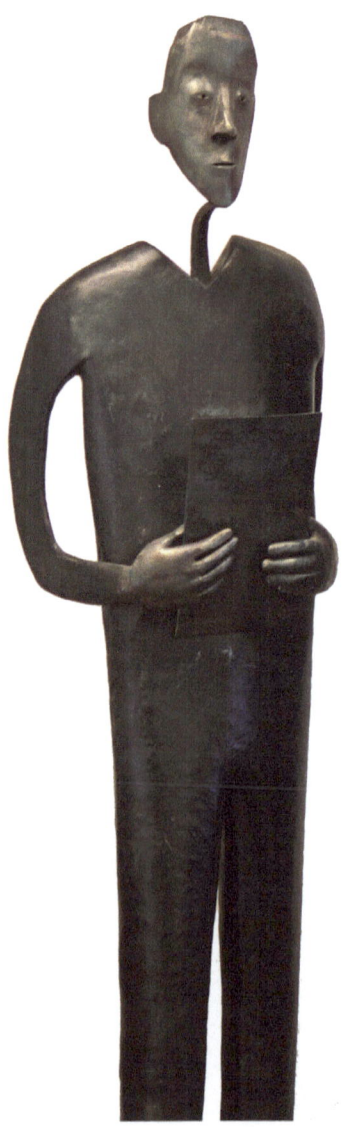

But the need for information
is overrated. A doughnut does
not taste any better knowing
the inner thoughts of the baker.

But a good title is never wrong.

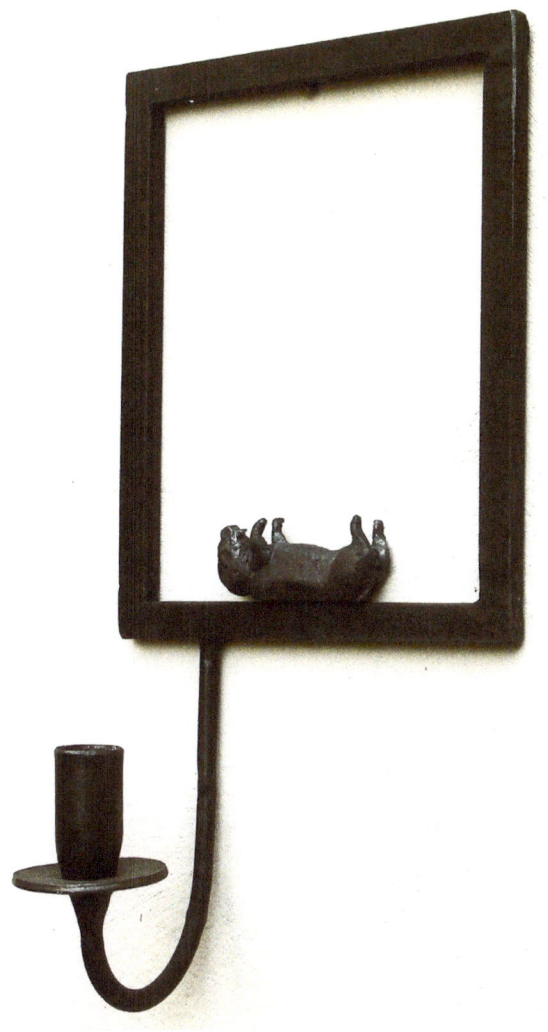

in memory of a dead hamster

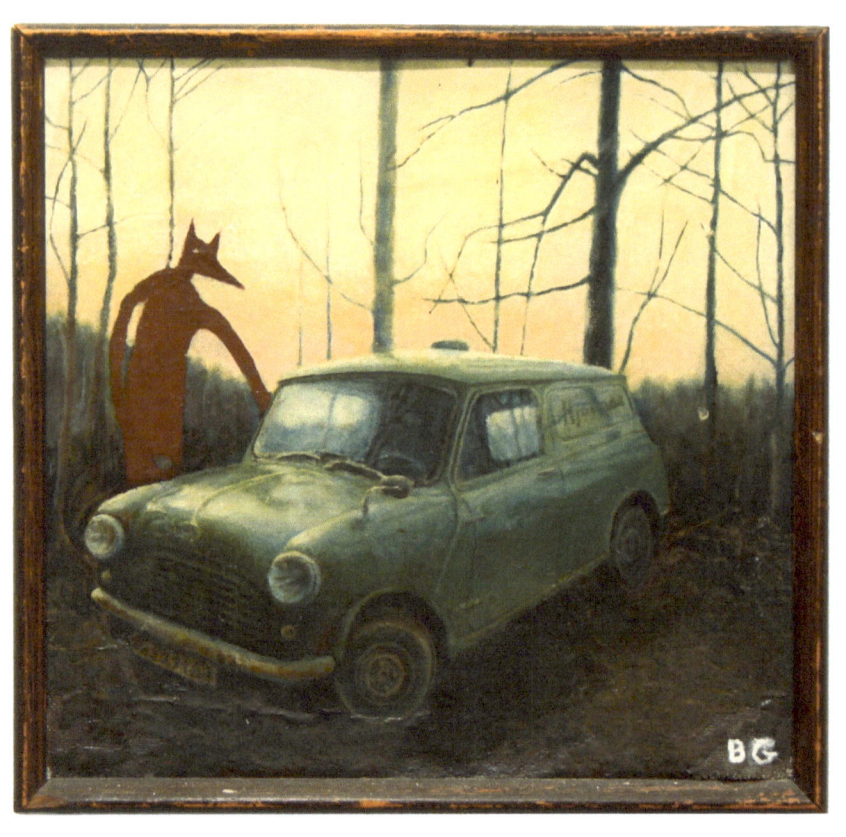

Fox and a mini cooper

Sometimes things that looks like
Art is art, sometimes it´s not.
Sometimes you´re just standing there
looking at some cheap copy.

It all depends on the context. Knowing
where the world of Art ends and
where the real world begins is difficult.
Not to mention who´s a real Fine Artist
and who is not. You need at least a
bachelors degree in Arts to really grasp
it, and even then you wouldn´t be sure.

In reality this is not a major problem.
There is hardly any money in it for
most of the artists and if you don´t get
touched you can always stop looking.

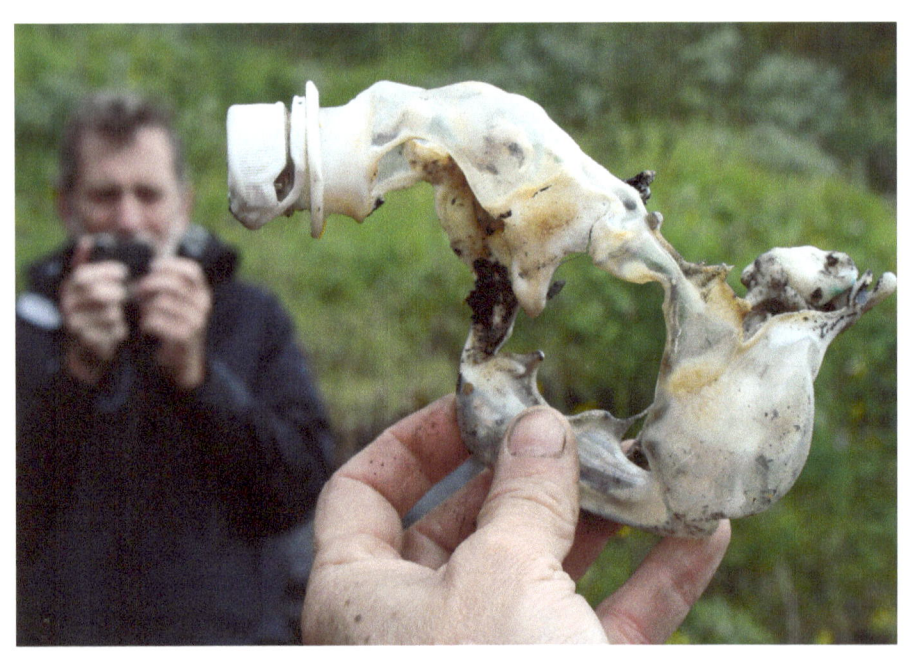

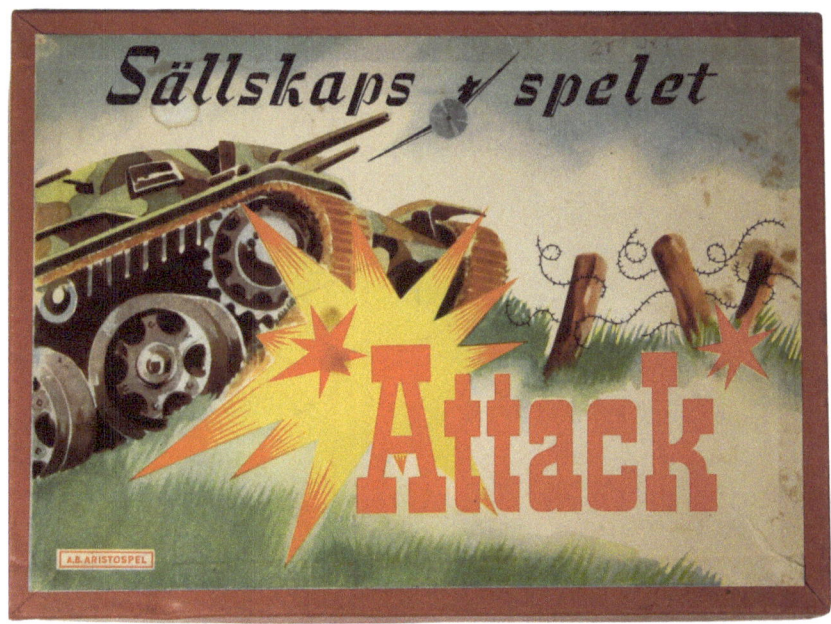

The parlour game "Attack"

There are things that unintentionally looks like Art. Things that just pop up and seem to have something to say.

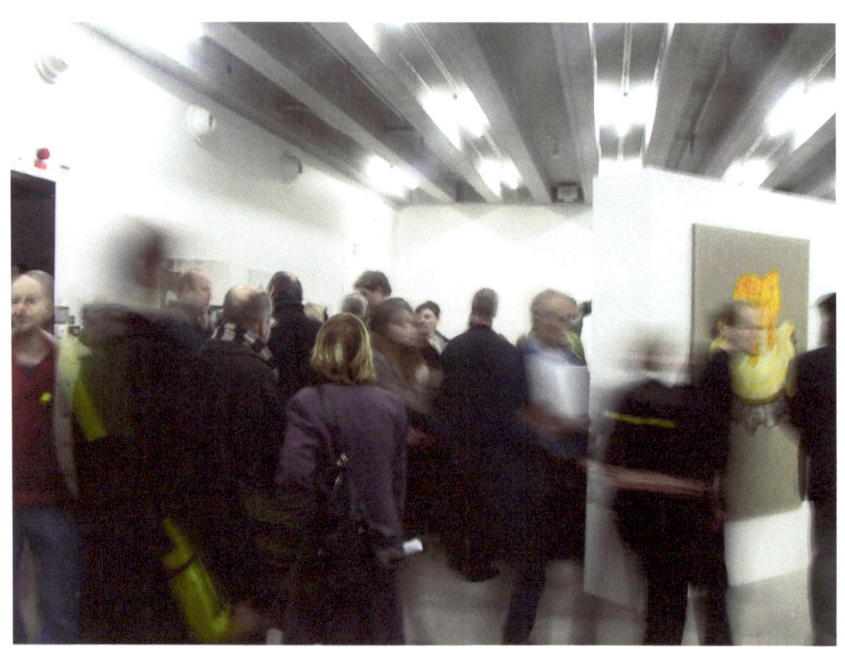

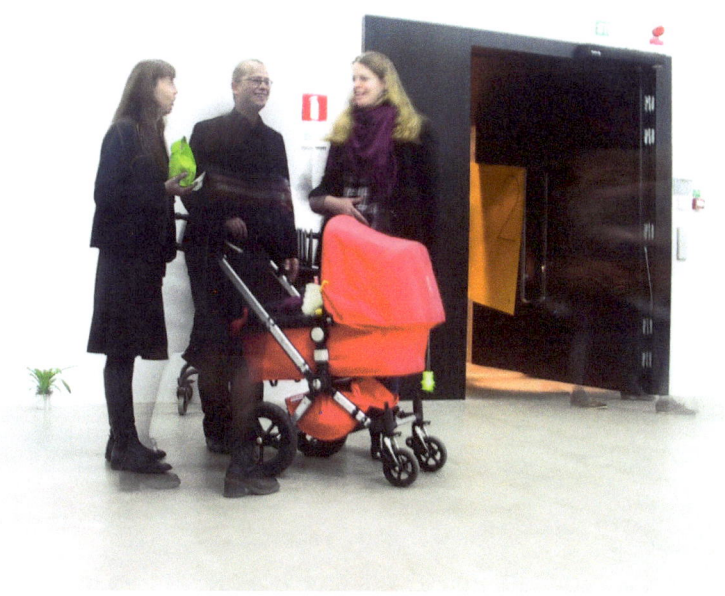

But most things that looks like Art
are found in art-galleries.
There you also find the people that
looks at things that looks like Art.
Sometimes they too look like Art.

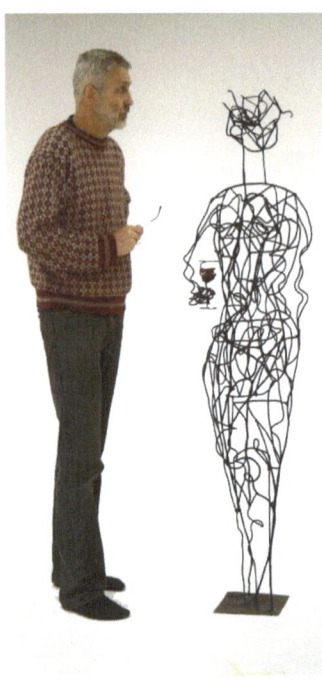

Vernissage is a little like graduation-day for those who do things that looks like Art. Friends and relatives show up. People from Art unions and those who also do things that looks like Art.

They all gather to mingle, drink a few glasses of wine and feel like they are a part of the local art scene.

And then they want to know how you think. For this there are different strategies:

Either you talk about which technique you´ve used or else you loose yourself in some obscure theory you have stumbled upon, letting it all end in a mumbling nothing.

"To this exhibition I choosed to work with an ESAB Mig-welding set and two DeWalt anglegrinders. With the 5"discs. And my sledgehammer of course. Then I changed shielding gas to a smoother sort that gave less spirt but soon realized I had to go back to the older one. It felt more direct...
And the slips I made while grinding was left as part of the process. A way of showing the fragility of life you know...
Like the flies in a still-life."

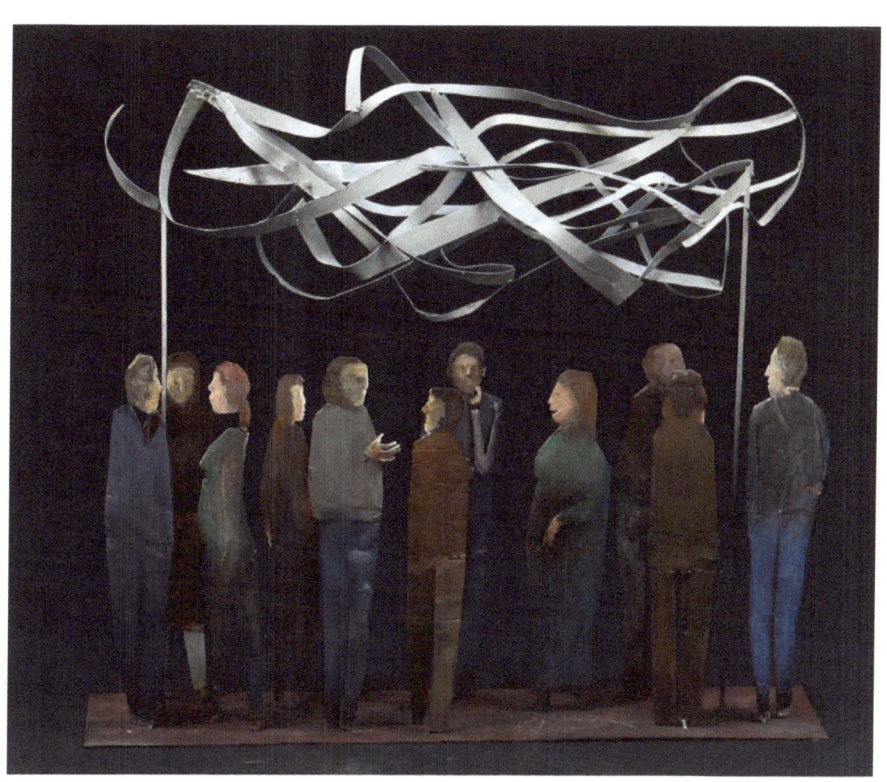

The main thing is to meet the
expectations of how a real artist
behaves. A real artist drinks
wine and speaks in riddles.

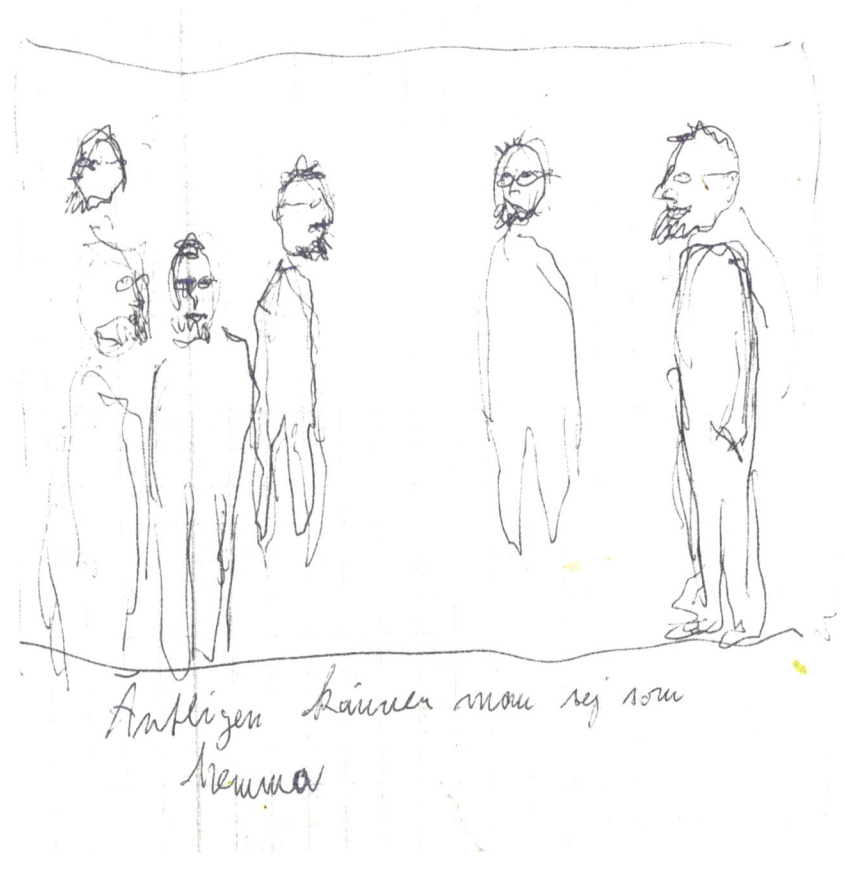

Finally I feel at home

Doing things that looks like Art is a lonely occupation. You´re the only one that fully comprehends what you´re trying to express. The world of Arts consist of solitaries who look upon everybode else as figurants, and in the meantime desperately seeks their recognition.
No wonder exhibition organizers are called curators.

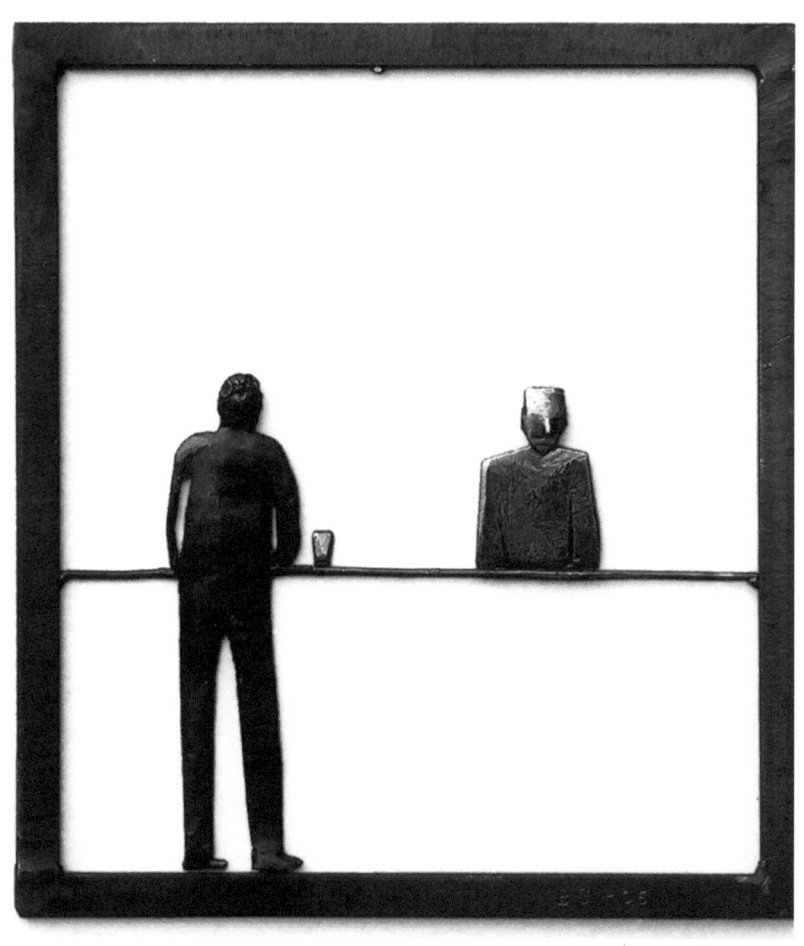

An evening out

Devaluation

Talking to a music journalist. He has trouble surviving. There are so many blogs about music that no one is willing to pay for reviews. One in a row of complaining culture workers, culture is a hard way to make a living. In a way it´s due to the fact that when a phenomenon loses it´s exclusivity it also drops in value. What everybody can do is no longer a skill you can get paid for.

This is also the case with pictures. Nowadays everybody takes pictures and put on the net. We get drenched in images and many of our viewer impressions are digital. We copy and manipulate which affects our perspective. Pictures gets devaluated

One answer is like a jongleur increase the degree of difficulty. Joggle with burning sticks or strawberry cakes. On a festival I saw a fiddler, in horsetail and a polka dot dress, play a whirling solo while seemingly without effort tap dance in pace. The tapdance didn´t contribute that much to the music but we all burst out in cheers. Everybody loves virtuosity.

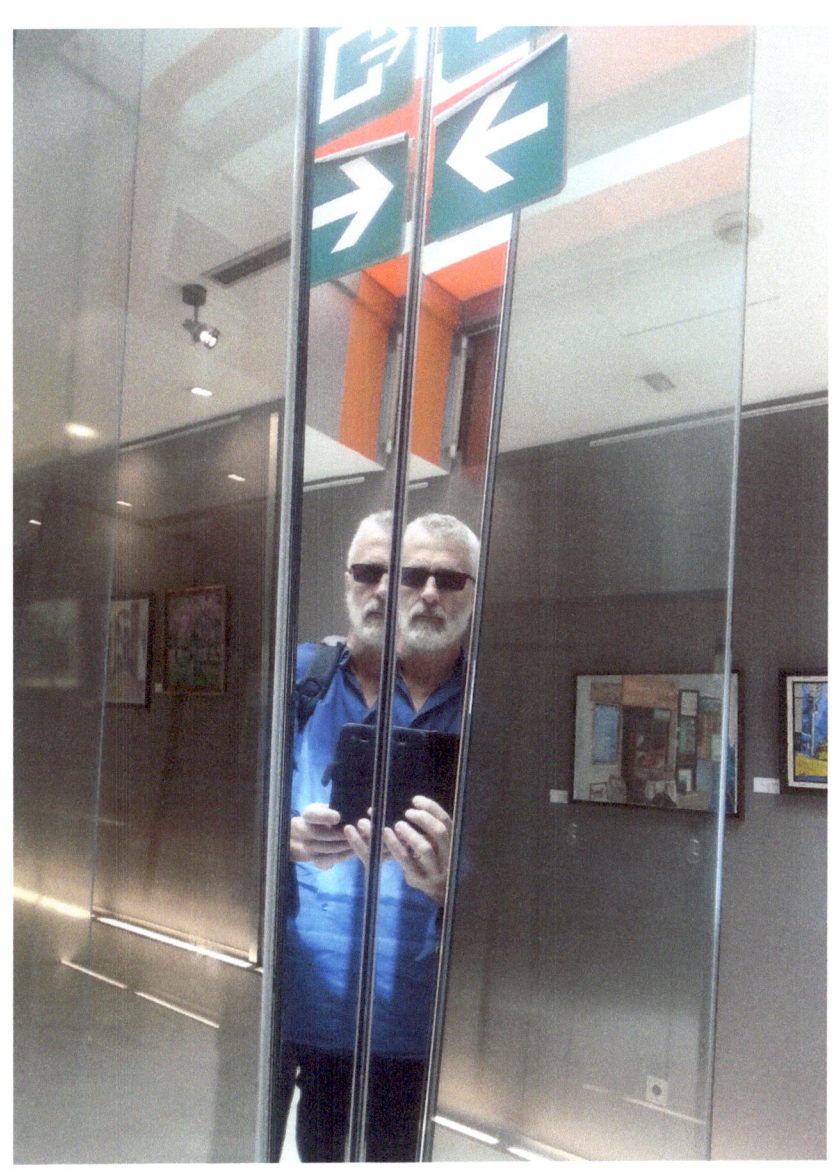

In Auckland Art-museum I once saw a piece made by William Kentridge using increased degree of difficulty. It was one of his usual charcoal animations but this time done so the only way to interpret it was through a polished stainless cylinder. Skilled and cool but not new. I had seen it done before. In a piece from the 18 century, shown at the Tromp d´oeil exhibition at the National Museum in Stockholm 2008.

Phantasmagoria: Byzantine and Gothic ornamentation. The woodcarving and tattooing of the Maori culture. The triple hirrients in hard rock solos. All these highly skilled digressions, not necessarily beautiful but always impressive. I don´t know what the music critic should do to increase his degree of difficulty.
Do his writing blindfolded?

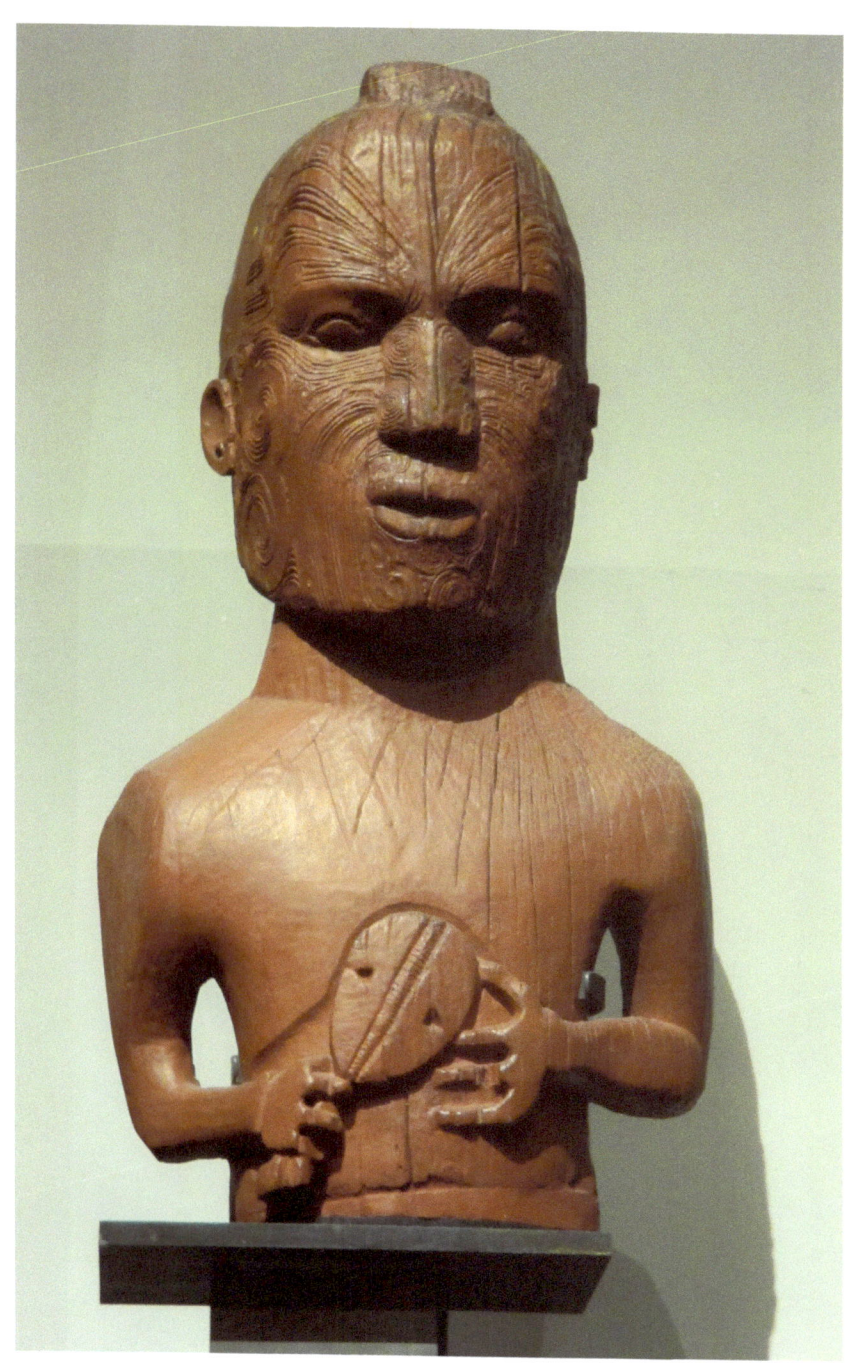

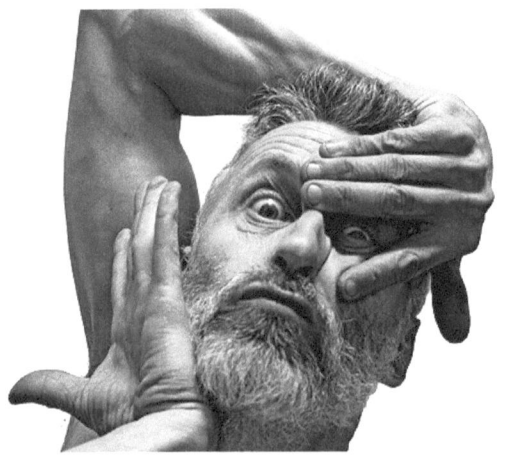

Another answer is highbrowing. Doing things so inaccessible they become reserved to a educated elite. Narrow the market to those who count and leave the rest unmoved.

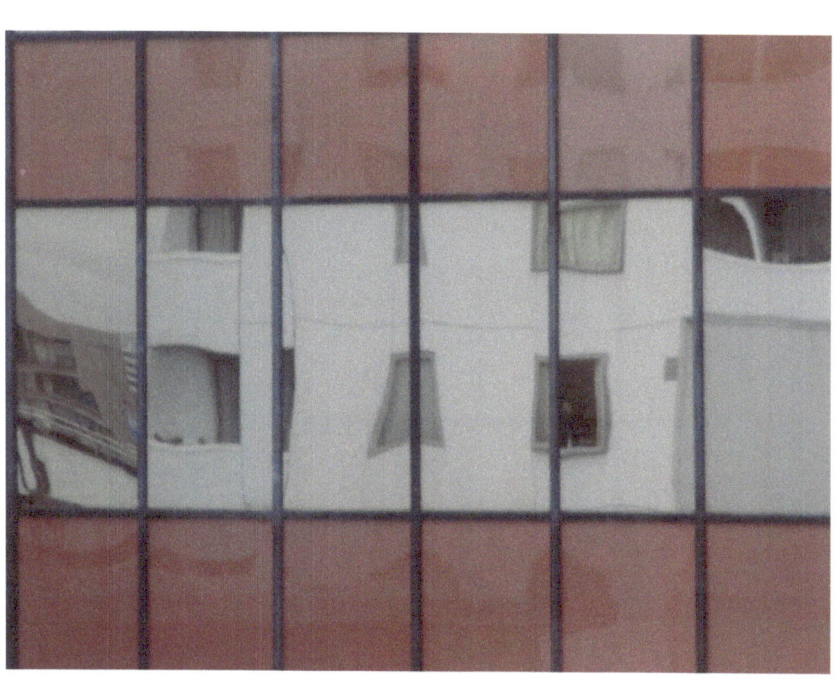

The anonymous entrance. The indifferent gallery owner, who with a single glance rules you out as a non-potential buyer and returns to her surf pad. The impenetrable text masses and implicit references you have get in to fully understand the items displayed. Items that under different circumstances would be passed with a shrug. Highbrowing is a self increasing mechanism that makes everyone involved feel important.

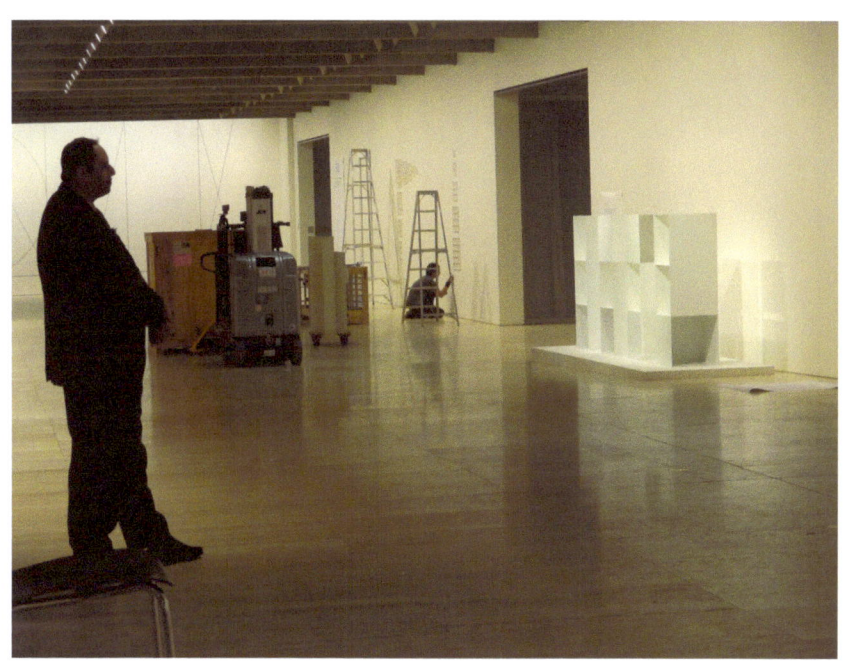

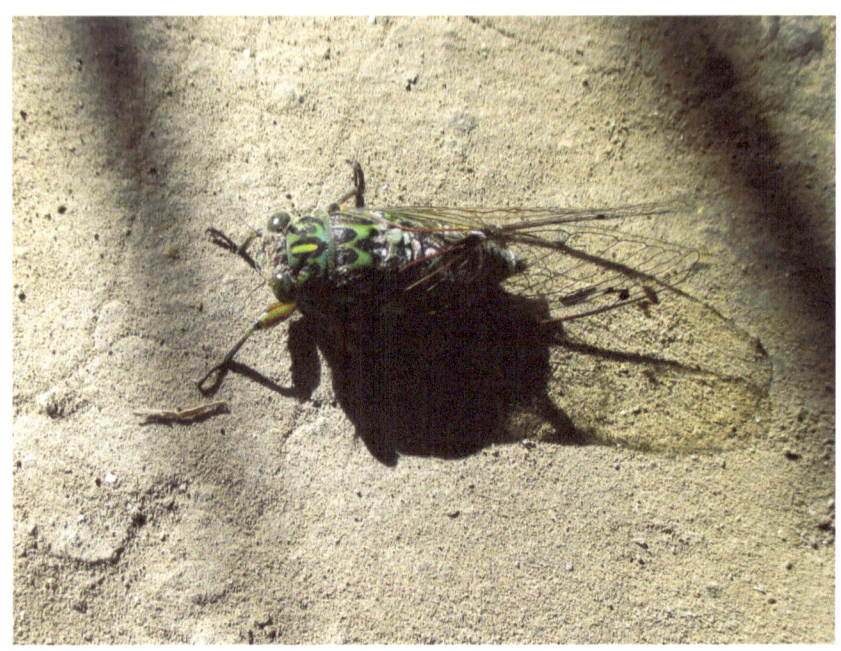

Follow a sparsely cleared trail, bow under branches
and palm leaves. Walk in a nature reserve on Waiheke
Island. The cicadas squeak och I scare away a couple of
big birds. They disappear with a turmoil among the trees
before I can see what they look like.
"*Commodity fetishism*" grinds in my head like a mantra.
Think about the role Fine Art plays in the late capitalistic
society and find that old Marxist terms from my youth
still feels up to date. The tendency that more and more of
human activity is sucked into a swirling commodity-carousel.
Emptied of it´s real content and reduced to simple objects of
Buy and Sell. That this also applies to the works of Art.
Commodity fetishism- Reification - Alienation.
The cicadas snap their legs in consent.

Sweden is moving from Public supported culture to a more Market adjusted. From municipal music schools to Idol. What kind of culture this will effect in is yet to be shown. There is at least a renaissance for Maecenas in view of all recently opened private museums.

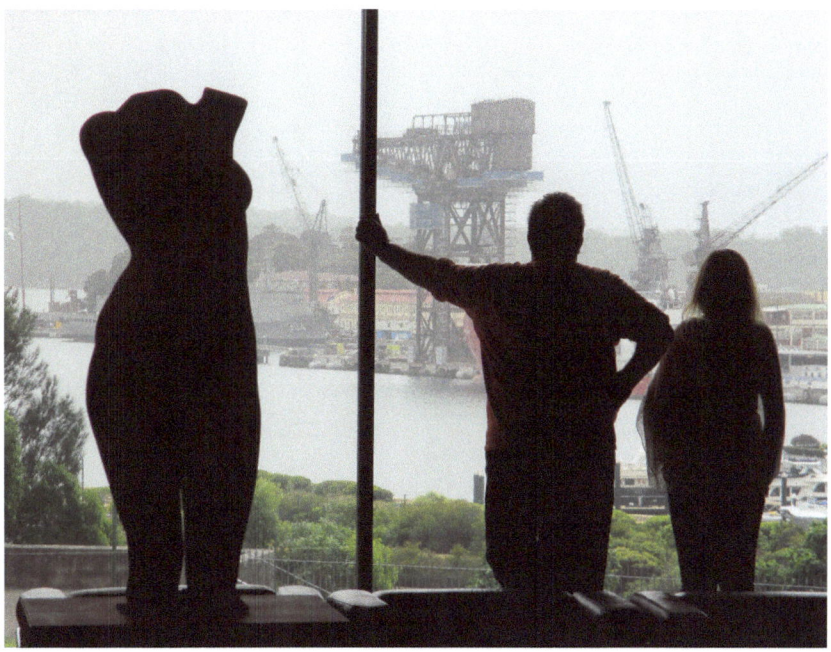

DOUBT

Doubt is a sound reaction. Without doubt no ideas will sharpen. Without doubt you become a second rater. Doubt is a key-component when making things that looks like Art.

But you also have to believe. Believe in yourself. Believe in the field you are working in and in your ability to realize your visions. Solely doubt makes you cynical and leads to bad self esteem. Balancing between hubris and paralysis is an endless story.

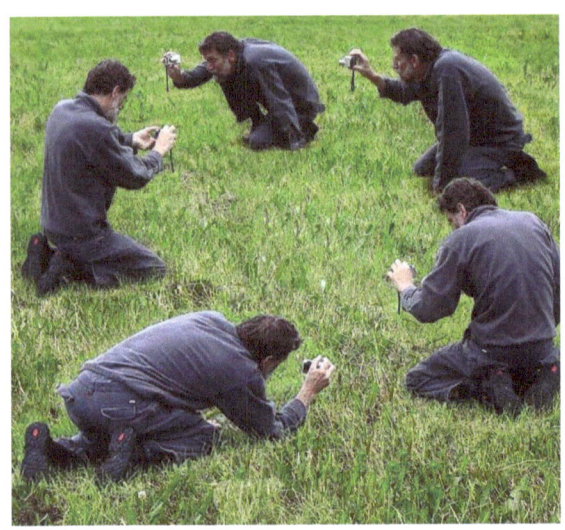

The Art world is often accused of being self-centered. This is true and it´s partly because Fine Arts role in society has changed. Much of it´s former assignments is now carried out by advertising agentcys. The market for battle-pieces and royal portraits has declined. Art of today is more to be seen as a phenomenon in the outskirts of entertainment industry.

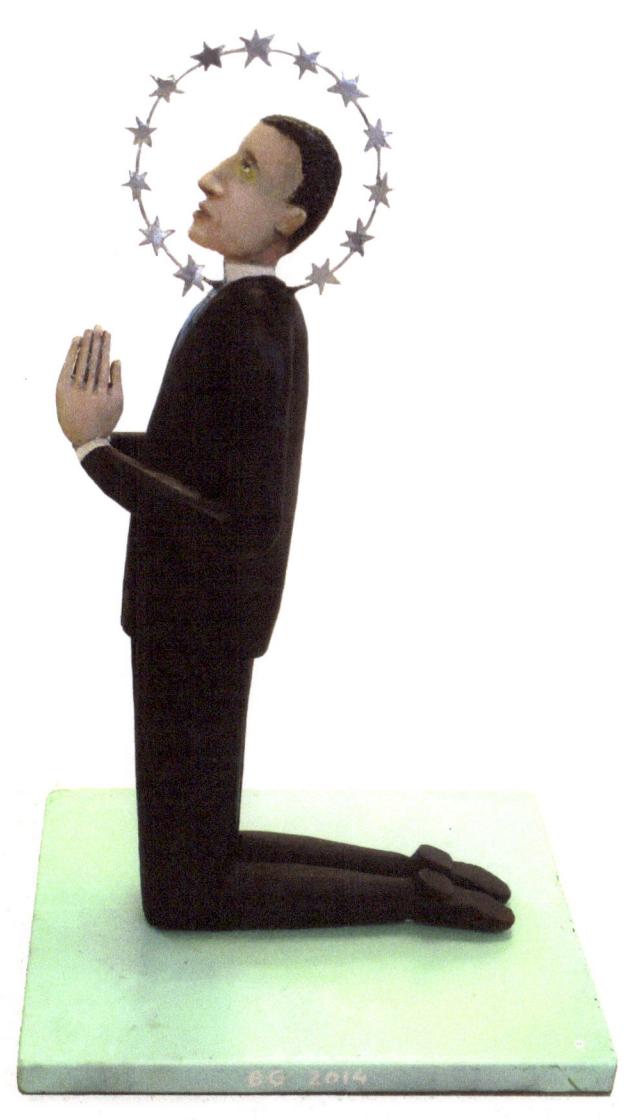

Even so, you still can find examples of homiletic art.

That brings us to the question of the usefulness of Art. Some things that looks like Art can possibly be used as fruit plates or candy bowls.

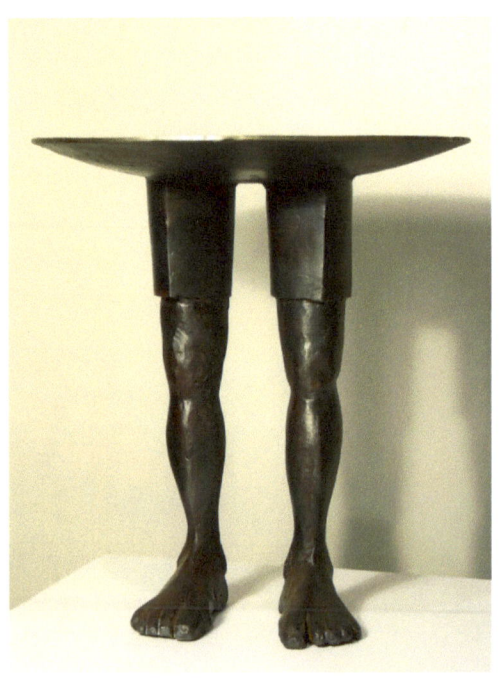

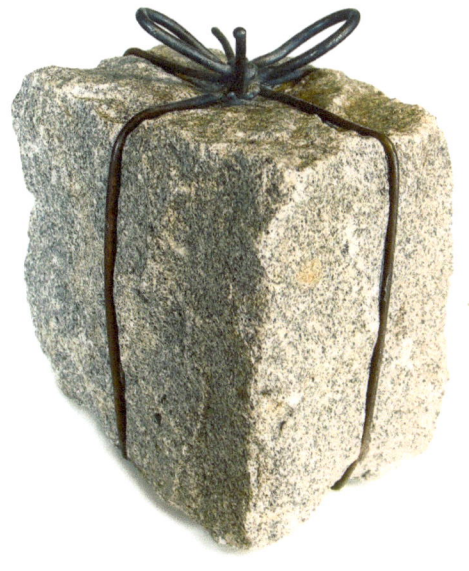

But most things have no practical benefit. They are only to be looked upon. Their value is of the same kind as the buzz of a bumblebee in a summer meadow.

Useful Art is often boring.
Best is the one that just is.

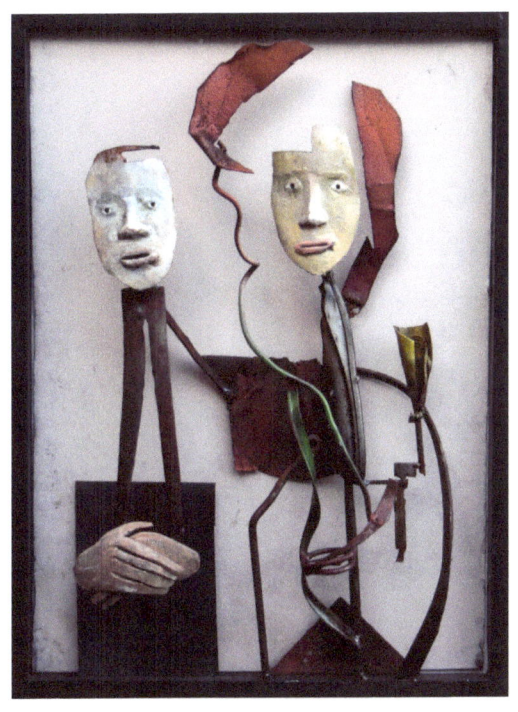

*We hear what you're saying but
you still can't go to that festival.*

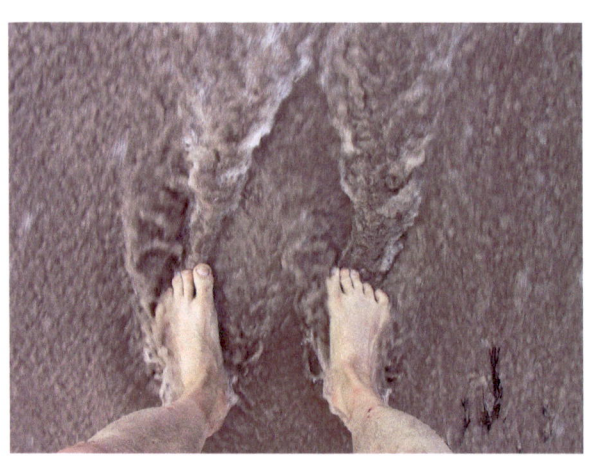

Any deep thoughts these lines or pictures have inflicted are totally unintentional and solely depends on the readers own assumptions.

Sundsvall 2014
Björn Gimstedt

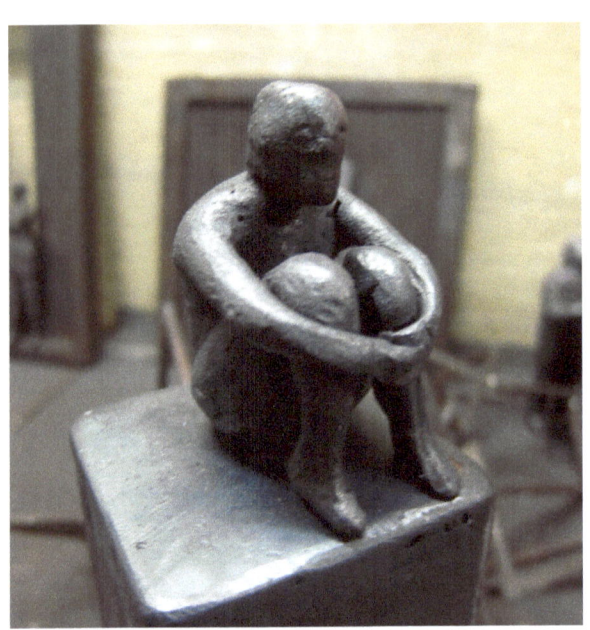

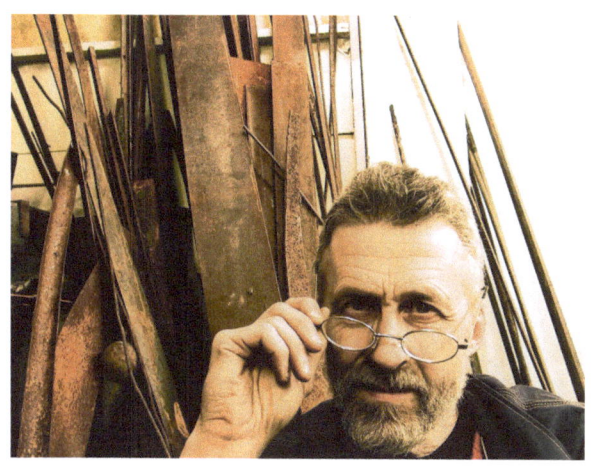

Björn Gimstedt, Born 1953.
Swedish Artist, Musician and Craftsman.
Live and work in Sundvall, a small town in the north of Sweden.
Also present on the net: *www.gimstedt.se*

Copyright and photo: Björn Gimstedt

www.ingramcontent.com/pod-product-compliance
Lightning Source LLC
Chambersburg PA
CBHW041942240526
45473CB00033B/414